BLACK PEARLS BEFORE SWINE

poems

L. A. Beckwith

Copyright © 2012 L. A. Beckwith
All rights reserved.

ISBN: 0615613594
ISBN-13: 9780615613598

laBeckwith.com

Table of Contents

Acknowledgment	vii

I. Looking Back

Crown of Glory	2
We Are Human	5
Curiosity	6
Twin Scourge	8
Medgar Evers	11
Rent Party	12
Conversing with the Wind	14

II. A Poets Point of View

Troy Davis	18
911	20
Mr. President	21
Hurricane	23
For Us	25
Haiku #2	26
Recipe for Recession	27
Two Piece	28

III. All of the Things in Between

New Money	32
Aunt Lucy	34
I Like Being Me	35
Leaving Room	37
Haiku #1	38
Symphony of the City	39
Free to Be	40
Wishful Thinking	42
Still Waters	43

IV. On Love and Loss

At Long Last	46
Disappearing Act	52
Just to Keep My Mind off You	53
Miracle	54
Foolish	55
Love Poem	56
Home	57
No Words	59
Give Me More	60

V. Obituary Blues

Paradise	62
Save Room in Heaven	63
We'll Remember You (for Tim-Tim)	64
Be with the Lord	65
In Memoriam	66
Don't Bring Roses	67

VI. Hope Is on the Horizon

On the Line	70
Out of Sight	71
Peace	74
Promised Land	75
Frankie	77
Keep Talking	80
Happiness	81
Never Give Up	82
Tracks	83
Breaking Point	87
The Future Is Watching	88

Acknowledgment

I cannot thank you enough for supporting this book. It has always been a dream of mine to publish a book of poetry and I am beyond thrilled to have this dream fulfilled. This collection of poetry was written between 1998 - 2012 and is a true account of my personal experiences over the years that I am now sharing with you. It also includes a journey to times past, my views on the social and political landscape, love, hope and so much more. I want to especially thank my mother, Doreen Beckwith and everyone who has inspired and encouraged me throughout the years. Your positive feedback motivated me to continue writing even when other things in my life had become a higher priority. I soon realized that those things were merely distractions and that writing should be my main focus. I hope that after reading, you will be enlightened, moved or even simply entertained. Finally, I'd like to dedicate this book to Terry Christopher Lee. You are a Godsend and I am forever grateful.

I.
Looking Back

Crown of Glory
(2007)

You may only see a head full of gray hair
But I call it my platinum crown of glory
And the wrinkles on my face
Could tell the most amazing stories
You've ever heard
When I speak, people hang on to every single word
Because I have lived

As part of the Great Migration
We fled the Confederation
For better compensation
In the land referred to as Black Mecca
And after a brief decadence
Emerged the arts, intellectual and literary movement
Called the Harlem Renaissance
Offering a sophisticated ambiance
Where black thought was embraced
We wrote, played and sang
About the challenges we faced
And the majority couldn't deny that we had skill
Zora and I were tit for tat (if you will)
And Louis taught me how to scat

Black Pearls Before Swine

Long before the record deal
Decades later, came the Civil Rights Movement
Triggered by the death of Emmet Till

In those days, we never simply stood still
We moved until our quality of life improved
I crossed the Mason-Dixon line
And traveled back to my roots
I participated in every boycott
Strapped up my boots
And marched next to King and Coretta Scott
We peacefully demonstrated
Causing buses and schools to be desegregated
I even supported the four that sat-in day after day
Until they were finally served at the diner in Carolina

Because of our efforts the Civil Rights Act was passed
Followed by the Voting Rights Act
Which eliminated the poll tax
I can go on and on, but I've taken this stroll back
As far as my memory will allow
I have paid my dues and for you the time is now
What stories will you have to tell
There's a leader in you waiting to be unveiled
And after your work is done
And you are fortunate enough
To live as long as I

Then you'll understand why the wrinkles on my face
And the gray hair on my head
I wear with dignity and grace
Because you too, will know what it means to live

Black Pearls Before Swine

We Are Human
(2011)

We are human
Just of another hue, man
Denied the right to a formal education
And we still became Martin, Malcolm and Huey Newton
Why do your hearts harbor hate?
Why do you defame and berate?
Then call us monkeys as justification
Placed us in trees as strange ornamentation
Fed us your religion
As a means of social order
Prayed to your God
While you preyed on our daughters
How contradictory
The world sees through your lies and trickery
We are people
Still haunted by the ghost of ole man James
Created in the likeness of the Almighty
So call us by our names

Curiosity
(2011)

They found my school books
Scattered along an old dirt road
Three days had passed
Since mama saw me last
And she lied in bed as still as
The weeping willow outside her window

I wish that I'd listened to mama's warning
But I could never resist the way
My loves pale skin glistened in the sun
Every morning
And she loved me sweetly
Although, discreetly
We dreamt of a place
Where we could be one freely

But someone caught wind to us
And put an end to us
She cried rape
I tried to escape

Black Pearls Before Swine

My body was found deep in the woods
Men wearing white robes and white hoods
Beat me viciously, then hung my corpse for all to see
Some folks say, it was curiosity that killed me

Twin Scourge
(2007)

Beauty will get you in the door
But your brain will keep you
Beauty will get you in the door
But giving good brain won't keep you
See, I knew long before
Game and 'Ye professed, "You wouldn't get far"
That I didn't have to get undressed
To be a star
Mr. Radio man you know who you are
I won't call letters
'Cause my mother taught me better
Needless to say
I didn't get the position
Unfortunately, some sistahs
Are okay with sexual favors being in the job description
But, I guess they don't know their history
'Cause if they did
They would know that black women
Have been using sex for centuries
Not just for personal gain
Back then, we would give our bodies
In exchange for merely

Black Pearls Before Swine

The basic necessities of our families
For our husbands to be treated less severely
A hit with the master's back hand
Instead of a closed fist
Black women, we were paying with our bodies
To simply exist

The conclusion of being a woman and black
This fusion of race and gender
Resulted in us having to surrender ourselves sexually
And these events caused some of us
To believe subconsciously
That through sex was the only way to succeed
And this is how some of our
Sexual principles came to be
So now that we've made the connection
Can we make the correction?
It could all be so simple
Understand that your body is your temple
And our foremothers didn't have a choice
But thanks to them we do
And this is for my black men too
We helped you by getting into
Those exploitative positions
So now that you're in authoritative positions
Can you give a deserving sistah a break?
And stop trying to take advantage of the situation

Black women, let's get rid of this negative reputation
Cause we really don't have to give head to get ahead
And if that door was meant for you to walk through
You wouldn't have to stoop so low

Medgar Evers
(2011)

Oh, dear Medgar
I have carried this name
In shame
And long to sever
The ties that bind
Your killer and I together

Rent Party
(2011)

My landlord's 'bout to give me the boot
On account that I'm behind on rent
'Cause I ain't got loot
I'm throwin' a party
And if my neighbors complain
I won't give a hoot
Once they smell the pigs feet cookin'
They'll soon follow suit
So come alone, bring a friend
Or you can even bring a date
Just ring bell number seven
When you get to the gate
A half-dollar at the door
And twenty five cents a plate
A jug full of moonshine
Will surely set you straight
'Cause cheap liquor
Will get you bent much quicker
Just look at Cecil Brown
Gettin down and dropped his knickers!
Tryin' to outdo Leroy and Tom
And Skinny Jimmy

Black Pearls Before Swine

I ain't never had a better time
Doin' the Black Bottom, Cake Walk
And the Shimmy
The next morning, my landlord's
At my door with his hand out
Saying, "Gimme!"
To his surprise, I gave him
Every dime, nickel and penny

Conversing With the Wind
(1998)

Maybe it was my imagination
But I heard it speak to me
And without hesitation
I regarded eagerly

It spoke of the original man
That first inhabited the Earth
And spoke of the original woman
Who was the first to give birth

It spoke of how we were seized
And taken without question
It spoke of how we were diseased
And forced into oppression

It spoke of all the ships
That we were placed upon
It spoke of all the whips
That beat us 'til the dawn

It spoke of how we got lost
In the hells of the USA

Black Pearls Before Swine

It spoke of us paying the cost
Of just living from day to day

It spoke of how God has arrived
To correct the wrongs of our oppressors
It spoke of how still, we survived
Though we were made to feel lesser

It spoke of writing down our history
Before we are erased
It spoke of us becoming a mystery
Being wiped out as a race

It spoke of teaching wisdom of self
And not only teaching belief
It spoke of us gaining back our wealth
And being in a state of relief

I asked one question - "Why?"
We had suffered for so long
But the wind did not reply
Then the breeze grew strong

And I looked around with fright
As it rustled through the trees
I'll never forget that night
Of speaking with the breeze

II.
A Poets Point of View

Troy Davis
(2011)

Have you heard about that Georgia boy?
Last name Davis, first name Troy?
Mama Virginia's pride and joy?

Folks said he killed a man
Testified on the witness stand
Swore on the Bible with their hands

No scientific evidence
A reasonable doubt, a cloud of suspense
Not one juror on the fence

When seven out of nine
Changed their minds
A petition for a retrial was declined

No justice, now two victims dead
Two families, with one common thread
"I'm innocent" is all Troy ever said

Black Pearls Before Swine

America the beautiful, is an ugly lie
How many more men will wrongfully die?
While we shamefully stand idly by?

911
(2001)

While you were pulling brothas over
For banging music in their jeeps
They were the ones catching cabs
In the city that never sleeps

While you were pulling brothas over
For rocking 'locs and wearing cornrows
They were the ones plotting and scheming
Walking around in normal folks clothes

While you were pulling brothas over
'Cause they fit a description
They were the ones taking flight lessons
Without any suspicion

While you were pulling brothas over
For simply being a brotha
They were the ones that caught you slippin'
Now ain't that a mutha?

Mr. President
(2011)

President, President,
Where are the weapons of mass destruction?
Why did you put innocent lives at risk
with your lies and blatant corruption?

President, President,
Why did you discourage peaceful negotiations?
Your dangerous political philosophies
Left us hated by countless nations

President, President,
Why did you drag your feet with Katrina
and leave thousands of people desperately waiting
to only be cheated and neglected by FEMA?

President, President,
Why did you cater to the filthy rich
and allow the dwindling U.S. economy
to be run right into the ditch?

President, President,
Why didn't you ever find Osama?
Maybe too many days of rest and relaxation
Thank goodness for President Obama

Hurricane
(2008)

Hurri, cane is coming!
Declaring four hundred years of war
When billions of dollars have already been spent
And could've gone to a healthcare system for
The middle-class and poor

Hurri, cane is coming!
And wants to un-do Roe vs. Wade
A clear indication of a dismal future
Reversing a law that's granted women the choice
For over two decades

Hurri, cane is coming!
Searching for new areas to drill oil
Instead of exploring alternative methods
Like solar and wind energy right here on American soil

Hurri, cane is coming!
And wants to build more and more jails
When our education system lacks adequate funding
The former leader of the world, now watches China excel

Hurry, McCain is coming!
But he was forced to scale down the convention
Ironically, due to a hurricane in New Orleans
Some might call it divine intervention

A hurricane is coming, ya'll!
To the same city the Republican party so shamefully ignored
Those who think that it's coincidental
Have mercy on their souls dear Lord

For Us
(2012)

This is not for the elite
This is for the streets
For crooked corners on city blocks
Where agony meets defeat
For dreams shattered at first breath
For grim lives
And premature deaths
For the disenfranchised
And those set up to fail
For empty school yards
And overcrowded jails
For homes, broken beyond repair
For young boys and girls
Whose fathers were just not there
This is for my people
Beautiful, brilliant, resilient and strong
Armed with the emotional fortitude
To keep pushing along
For those who've overcome
Despite what the world has given
And continue to lead a life
That is virtuous and purpose driven

Haiku 2
(2011)

My sweet home is gone
The Man forced us to the 'burbs
Gentrification

Recipe for Recession
(2011)

In a large bowl
Pour in a generous amount of power
Add a handful of gluttony
Mix well and boil for an hour
To create greed
Then, add an unequal distribution of wealth
A dash of capitalism
A pinch of poverty for flavor
To achieve the taste of poor health
Lightly stir, then simmer five minutes
Place contents into a metal pan
Add two cups of diced deregulation
A hint of drained pension plans
A dollop of unemployment
Then sprinkle a little predatory lending
Bake twenty minutes at 500 degrees
Watch it burn to a crisp
Eat at your own risk

Two Piece
(2012)

Crispy, original
Spicy or mild
I've been crazy 'bout you
Since I was a child
A southern comfort on
A Sunday afternoon
With my fingers as utensils
Who needs a fork or spoon?
My love dates back to the days
Of tireless slaving
When only you could satisfy
My constant, insatiable craving
A good ole' source of protein
Kept my body strong and lean
The love for your scrumptious taste
Must be planted in my genes

But somewhere along the way
You began to systematically advance
Greedy industry leaders found ways
To chemically enhance your growth speed
By putting hormones in your feed

Black Pearls Before Swine

But your taste was never compromised
Though, you were obviously bigger in size
Then, the result of your unnatural makeup
Began to take effect on our lives
Like, little girls' bodies developing faster
Than their minds
They don't know how to handle the attention
From having big breasts and big behinds
And then their risk for breast cancer
Becomes much greater
When they reach puberty sooner rather than later
So what is the solution, buying organic?
Well, that might be quite difficult
For Blacks and Hispanics
When economics is the reason why
We indulge in the first place
Somehow it always seems
To come down to race

III.
All of the Things in Between

New Money
(2011)

Sugar, I've seen new money before
I know exactly how it looks
Big screen TVs and oversized furnishings
Stuffed in every cranny and nook

Baby, I know just how new money tastes
I've dined the most lavish restaurants
So save your lobster tails and caviar
For some ole wide-eyed debutante

Honey, I know the smell of brand new money
I recognize the scent
Fresh leather interior of foreign luxury coupes
I've probably paid more in rent

Darling, I know what new money sounds like
An assortment of braggadocios drivel
About where you've been and what you have
You couldn't be more anti-civil

Black Pearls Before Swine

I know how new money feels, sweetie
It's sizzling hot to the touch
Go ahead and spend it as fast as you made it
But chile, that don't impress me much

Aunt Lucy
(2011)

My Aunt Lucy never liked me
Not even as a tot
Sometimes I think she hates me a little
Sometimes a lot

My Aunt Lucy loves misery
That's why she's always lonely
She smiles in my face, then stabs me in the back
She is the epitome of phony

My Aunt Lucy wishes bad upon me
Her heart is cold as winter
And whenever there is family friction
She's always at the center

My Aunt Lucy is crying for help
But conceals it as rancor
Her ill will motivates me to be the best
And for that, I'd like to thank her

I Like Being Me
(2011)

I am one tough cookie
But it took me a while to see
That I'm fine just the way I am
In fact, I like being me

Mister, I beg your pardon
If sometimes, I drink straight out of the carton
So what if I like to pick fresh herbs
Right from my neighbors garden

And if I wear a scarf to bed
To keep the kinks out of my head
I'm still a beauty queen, indeed
Regardless of what those magazines have said

And if I sing each and every song
That comes through the speakers
Dancing in the mirror
With nothing but my sneakers

It's alright with me
'Cause I like being me

And if I wanna stuff my face
With fried chicken, then say my grace
And take a little from your plate
Just 'cause I want a taste

Or if I wanna sleep 'til three
Get up and watch reality TV
Then get myself together
For a weekly shopping spree

And if I wanna change my hair
Along with all the seasons
I'll do just that
'Cause I'm not into pleasing

No one but me
'Cause I like being me

Leaving Room
(2010)

People remove themselves
From our lives
Sometimes, against our will
We didn't think we could be without them
But in time
All things heal
And in time
Answers are revealed
That empty space becomes filled
Then it's safe to assume
That they were simply leaving room

Haiku 1
(2011)

The sad brown girl cries
And prays that no one sees her
It rained for hours

Symphony of the City
(2011)

Some nights, I lie awake
Listening to the symphony of the city
The syncopated footsteps pounding pavement
The rhythmic chattering of crowds
The thunderous horns
The melodious moans of the destitute
And I wonder where they are going
Imagine what they are talking about
Ponder their hurry
Contemplate the source of their pain
And although I may never know these things
And our lives may never come into contact
We affect one another
In ways we may never know

Free to Be
(2011)

I called my boss this morning
And told him I was ill
I'm gonna skip that hell hole today
And do whatever it is I feel

Maybe I'll never go back again
Maybe I'll visit an old friend
In Harlem, New York or the South of France
Take a piano lesson
Or learn to belly dance

Maybe I'll get a vocal trainer
And start a brand new band
Cover a tune by Gloria Gaynor ("I Will Survive")
Or escape to a private island
And write the book that I've been putting off
For so long
About the things in my life and the world
That seems to have all gone wrong

Black Pearls Before Swine

Take my mom on a nice vacation
Learn a new language or two or three
Get a job at a radio station
Playing smooth jazz and R&B

Produce a documentary film
On black love on the West Coast
Or fall madly in love in the Windy City
With whomever I like the most

Or maybe I'll start a non-profit
For at-risk youth
Show them the way and inspire them to
Always seek the truth

Or I'll study theatre
And put on a one-woman show
Lend a hand in the Mother Land
And tell everyone I know

How nothing could ever come close
To the feeling of being free
And believe without a doubt
That I can do whatever I want
And be whatever I want to be

Wishful Thinking
(2011)

I've spent all these years hating you
While you were as happy as can be
Living a lovely fairytale life
With your wife and family

I hoped that somehow
You would feel my hate
And it would tear you up inside
I wanted to create a pain in you
That not even a smile could hide

Then a wise woman said
That I was wasting energy on someone
Who wasn't even thinking of me
So I focused that energy somewhere else
And used it more positively

Now, I hope the very best for you
And that Karma takes it light
But then again, I hope it comes around
And knocks you out with all its might

Still Waters
(2012)

I found you
Hiding behind religion
Pretending to be someone you are not
Afraid of revealing your true self
For fear of rejection
You strive for perfection
But it is outside of your reach
You do the opposite
Of what you preach
How do you sleep?
Knowing the pain that you caused
Runs deep
Just like still waters

IV.
On Love and Loss

At Long Last
(2007)

In the back of the ritzy lounge
Sat a handsome and dapper fella
She asked if she could have the seat next to him
And introduced herself as Estella
It was her grandmother's name
That she had finally grown into
It complemented every aspect of her style
He greeted her with a heartfelt smile
That stretched from ear to ear
And rivaled the Nile

He was about twenty years her senior
With a cool, jazz-like demeanor
You should have seen her
She was gone at hello
And if it were up to her
Good-bye would be a no-show
Her taste had always been of things retro
It was only natural that she'd be sweet on him
They carried conversations to the tune of
Love, music and spirituality
He said that he changed his life including his name

Black Pearls Before Swine

When he found God
By the way, his name was Ahmad
And even though he was down with
A seven and a crescent
She knew he was heaven sent
That could only explain why their bond
Was far beyond ordinary
There were two decades between their ages
But they found themselves on the very same pages

She finally realized what being patient really brings
For so many years, she'd been on a trek for love
But the moment she made the decision to wait
She'd be discovered by her mate
He looked deeply into her eyes
As if he was soul searching and said
"It feels like I've known you forever,
Are you sure we've never met?"
And she boldly returned, "I'm not that easy to forget."
He kissed her hand and she silently thanked the Creator
While he motioned for the waiter to close the tab
The night had come to an end, so he offered her a cab
And she accepted with ease
The temperature dropped to about twenty-two degrees
It was typical Chicago weather
Naturally, to keep warm, they nestled closer together
She'd never felt so secure in any other man's embrace

She lifted her head towards his face
It was almost as amazing as grace
That she could see herself and didn't need a mirror
Her image was unusually clearer
Her reflection was eternal in his eyes
Like moon-glow painted on lakes
Under nocturnal skies
Thoughts of love were premature
But it was a pure love, untainted
A familiar love, as if they'd met in another lifetime
And were getting reacquainted

They would be parting ways soon
Because the taxi had just arrived
He opened her door only to further remind her
That chivalry was still alive
She whispered, "It was nice to meet you."
And he replied, "The pleasure was all mine."
He asked if he'd be out of line
If he kissed her on the cheek
She answered with a smile and he said
"Close your eyes and don't peek."
It was the first time she'd ever felt tenderness
She opened her eyes and love no longer seemed bleak

On the ride home she couldn't stop thinking about
How the night was so incredible

Black Pearls Before Swine

While the song appropriately playing on the radio
Was Nat King Cole's "Unforgettable"
She only hoped that he thought of her in the same regard
Just before pulling up to her apartment on Jackson boulevard
She realized that he didn't inquire about keeping in touch
She grabs money from her leather clutch
To tip the driver and finds his card
He must have slipped it into her purse
She tips the driver a little extra
It was her way of paying back the universe

The next morning, she got out of bed
And opened the drapes in her kitchen
It was part of her morning tradition
To welcome in the sun
And revive her plants in the window
Yet, they were already full of zest
As to suggest that they didn't need the sun
The day had only just begun
But it was clear that it was going to be a good day
And without further delay
She called him
She didn't give much thought
To what she was going to say
He answered, "Hello Estella!"
It was like music to her ears only a cappella
He must have recognized it was her

Because the area code was from New York State
Before she could even say hello
He exclaimed, "I need to see you and it can't wait!"
She was delighted by his sense of urgency
He invited her to see
Roy Hargrove play downtown at eight

She wore her favorite dress
It was a black, satin dress with an umpire waist
Every single strand of her hair
Was perfectly in place
The ringlets of curls resembled flowers
The way they framed the side of her face
To chase away the butterflies, she shut her eyes
And kept them closed
Until she felt composed enough to walk in
He was sitting at a table in the corner
And he appeared to be happy to see her
But had a curious grin
He pulled out her chair and said
"Please sit down, I have something to tell you, but
I don't quite know where to begin."
Just as he's about to explain
He's greeted by an old friend
The man shouts, "Hello Dave!"
She thought that it was odd that
The man didn't refer to him as Ahmad

Black Pearls Before Swine

But she remembered that he changed his name
Though it never came up in conversation
That the old one was Dave
She started to think about everything from the night before
And it began to make sense
Maybe what they had in common
Was not a coincidence
The man asked, "Who is this lovely lady?"
Ahmad answered, "She's my lovely daughter."

Her eyes began to water
If her feelings were sound
They'd be reminiscent of the last breathe
Carried through a treasured horn
Composing imperfect notes that mourn loves demise
Love had come to a startling halt
She tried to find it in her heart
Not to place him at fault and learn to love him
Only this time as her dad
She didn't miss what she never had
There was no point in placing blame
The only thing she ever lacked
Was having his last name
He had everything, yet nothing to do
With the young woman she became
She asked, unromantically
"Where have you been all of my life?"

Disappearing Act
(2010)

I sleep 'til noon
But even that feels too soon
My heart's been singing
The same blue tune
Ever since he disappeared
Into the eventide
Searched for the answers
But the desire eventually died
No need in looking for the reasons why
I'll leave that to the Man in the sky
And in the meantime
I'll keep living

Black Pearls Before Swine

Just to Keep My Mind off You
(2006)

Tonight, I poured myself
A glass of wine
Heard Ella sing a line or two
Cleaned my house from top to bottom
Just to keep my mind off you

I glanced through some old photos
Tried on a lipstick in a different hue
Painted my finger nails and toes
Just to keep my mind off you

I primped in the mirror for a while
Recited my favorite poem too
Fixed my hair in a fancy up-do style
Just to keep my mind off you

I tried on my most desired clothes
Watched my favorite program too
Then thought about what I'd do tomorrow
Just to keep my mind off you

Miracle
(2008)

I've marveled at shooting stars
Impetuously competing against the moon
Watched a delicate butterfly escape
A silk cocoon

Saw a blind man paint a masterpiece
Capturing every shadow and light
I've even seen a single raindrop
Make a fading flower stand upright

This morning, I awoke early enough
To see the sun take its position in the sky
Boldly declaring the day anew
Though, I never witnessed a miracle
Until I laid eyes on you

Foolish
(2010)

You reached out and touched my feelings
Caressed my thoughts
And soothed my nerves
Promised that there was more
To this love
Than just my curves
We spoke in perfect harmony
Breathed in parallel rhythms
Then you transformed completely
With the swinging of the pendulum
You turned me into a memory
Tucked me away in the dull corners of your mind
Dimmed the light in my radiant eyes
Where love so foolhardily shined

Love Poem
(1998)

A constant notion
That enters my mind
I've searched for the potion
But still I can't find
A way to obtain
Your determined heart
I've endured plenty of pain
And I've been torn apart
As I gather up the scraps
From my hearts residue
The notion in my head entraps
Young man, that notion is you

Home
(2008)

It's no colossal house on the hill
Yet, it is still beautiful
Both inside and out
So attractive that it all but screams and shouts, "Welcome!"
A winding walkway adorned with blooming daffodils
Eased the lengthy passage to the door
Barely cracked open as if it were cautious of inviting strangers
She took her shoes off before entering
And tip-toed gently around the empty house
It hadn't been occupied for quite some time now
And she quickly imagined how she'd fill it with love
A sight to behold even with it's imperfections
Like the finger prints scattered on the red stained walls
The last residents' attempt to leave their mark, she thought
Rightfully, she simply wiped them away
Using only the sleeve of her shirt
It was clear that the former occupant had caused a little hurt
But she'd take special care
A fresh coat of paint here and there
A scent of lavender to fragrance the air
Overwhelmed with joy, she sat on the floor
And began to blissfully stare

At the four walls that made up the living room
The house, stripped of all the fancy dressings, felt like home
She made herself comfortable, unpacked her belongings
And promised to stay forever

No Words
(2010)

Don't speak
I can hear it
In your earnest embrace
No words from your mouth
Could satisfy the taste
Like a sweet caress
From your lips
On the tips of tongues of many
We find plenty of ways to illustrate
Your eyes fascinate me
With every display of devotion
I breathe you in and
I am filled with but one emotion
Love

Give Me More
(2011)

Give me more than
Just good looks and allure
Those things are sure to fade
I need something that in your absence
I wish that you had stayed

Make the darkness depart with your light
Make me thirst for your insight
Indulge me with expression

Give me more than
Just good love and appeal
Those things are real and true
I need something that in your presence
I'm given a fresh point of view

Show me the world through your eyes
Show me where truth lies
Inspire me with wisdom

V.
Obituary Blues

Paradise
(2011)

Beyond the blue horizon
Where the ocean meets the sky
Is a paradise I long to know
And angels sing on high

Vineyards flourish on fertile hills
And grapes in constant bloom
The garden of eternal bliss
Smells of sweet perfume

The life blood of the city sparkles
Dancing rivers flow without end
A quiet retreat so lovely and pure
Masterminds could not comprehend

Streets are paved in the purest gold
Walls are precious stone
An illuminated path leads the way
To our Savior on the throne

Black Pearls Before Swine

Save Room for Me in Heaven
(2008)

We surely lived a good life
What greater gift could a man receive
than a loving and devoted wife?

I thank the good Lord
For all fifty years
Of happiness, laughter and even the tears
For our children we made
Who loved us so dear
Though, in distance were far
But in spirit so near

They are constant reminders
Of your beauty and grace
Though the emptiness inside
Will never be replaced

Save room for me in Heaven
Because I'll save room for you
In my heart
Just to see you for a moment
From this ole Earth
I'd gladly depart

We'll Remember You (for Tim-Tim)
(2001)

We'll always remember your smile so serene
How your eyes lit all aglow
Your passion for art so intense, so keen
A gift we all came to know

We'll always remember your heart so true
Your willingness to give and share
Your determination to make it through
Even when it was hard to bear

We'll always remember your humor and wit
And all the love you had to give
Your precious memory we'll never forget
For as long as we all shall live

Be with the Lord
(2008)

Early one morning
I called out His name
Told Him I'm ready
And with angels He came

To take me to Heaven
And roam 'round all day
No worries, no pain
My troubles washed away

I trusted in the Lord
Now I have eternal bliss
Though loved ones and family
I will truly miss

When the burden gets too heavy
On the Almighty, you can depend
Keep your faith in the Lord
And I'll see you again

In Memoriam
(2005)

By his life we felt inspired
A smile that never grew tired
Through misfortune and even pain
His joyful spirit remained the same

Too large for worry, too strong for fear
Never signs of a falling tear
Tranquil, humble and especially wise
He deeply touched all of our lives

With a divine and loving essence
That brought such cheer
These are the memories our hearts
Will forever hold dear

Don't Bring Roses
(2011)

Don't bring me roses and other flowers
I can't appreciate them now
Don't weep for days or even hours
It won't bring me back anyhow

Just hug someone a little longer
The very next chance you get
Love someone a little stronger
Just like the first time you met

Call them every now and then
To make sure they're doing fine
Be the one who helps them when
They need a bit of sunshine

# VI.
Hope Is on the Horizon

On the Line
(2011)

Do you hear my liquid prayers?
Can you see me without all of the layers?
Do you know what's at my core?
Do you know me anymore?

Inevitably, I have changed
But in the process, I've become estranged
Though, life has brought me back on your course
Filled with shame, guilt and remorse

Make me as pure as winter snow
Give me the light and watch me grow
Bear with me now and in advance
Prepare to bestow a second chance

Out of Sight
(2007)

Between rocks and hard places
Maintain a smile like Pacs and Scarfaces
Opportunity knocks
No half steps, she races
And welcomes with wide open arms
No four leaf clovers or lucky charms
Could result in or come close
To what is already written by the Mos'
So, on faith, she takes tremendous leaps
Knowing that in His hands He keeps her safe
And her faith doesn't require sight
In her heart, He put the desire to fight
In her hand, He placed a pen
So that fire she writes
Hoping that when she recites
Their ears are open to receive
As she exclaims, His power is activated
Only when we believe
And sometimes it's hard to conceive
But just trust
'Cause He's guiding us in the best path
How many times in your life has direction followed rejection?

You do the math
To keep from crying she just laughs
Knowing that for every testing there's a blessing
Some in disguise
So she keeps pressing forward toward the prize
In preparation for the journey that lies ahead
It's a cold world but she ain't rocking
No leather bomber, instead
She's covered by His armor
Consequently, nothing can harm her
Though it ain't easy along the way
Nothing worth having is
And in this biz
It's hard to tell the wolves from the sheep
Do they really wanna help or just get in deep?
So she decides to categorize them all as snakes
Trying to make her compromise integrity
For big breaks
But she won't fold no matter how long it takes
Even if dreams come few and far between
Like catastrophic earthquakes
'Cause all life long she's been chasing waterfalls
Never settling for rivers and lakes
And ain't no way, no how
She'll ever throw in the towel
Not when He gave her the ability
To merge consonant with vowel

Black Pearls Before Swine

To formulate thought-provoking words on pages
To perform on stages
And inspire one spirit
The dream that once seemed so far
She finds herself near it

Peace
(2009)

In the sound of the blaring sirens
Between the angry, crashing waves
In the presence of the empty lions
Wherever Mother Nature misbehaves

On bloody battlefields of minds and matter
At the end of the rope swiftly fraying
On troubled hearts, hope begins to scatter
Somewhere near, tongues are fiercely praying

Though, a silent power already remains
In the very things causing destruction and despair
For in sorrow, calamity and pain
Peace rests so comfortably there

Promised Land
(2007)

I see the children running
Running quickly to the playground
As if they've found the Promised Land
They are running to the obstacle course of life
At break neck speeds
Where seeds have been planted
And pine trees grow rampant throughout the park
Oblivious of the journey for which they're about to embark

On swings, children are discovering their wings
In position to fly
Realizing that their strength will determine how high
They will soar

On the see-saw, children are learning the law of gravity
And that life is not without imperfection
Inevitably, it moves in an up and down direction

On monkey bars, children leap
Facing the challenge of having to keep one arm hanging freely
But they are strong
Understanding that courage will further them along

On the slide, children subside with the fear of falling
And are more likely to repeat
Believing that each time they go down
They will land on their feet

On the merry-go-round, children are learning
That without people turning, as with the world
It would simply stand still

I see the children running
Running quickly uphill to the playground
As if they've found the Promised Land

Frankie
(2007)

Frankie would kneel down every night to say his prayers
His grandmother constantly reminded him
To thank all of the naysayers
He was only three months shy of nine
But not old enough to wrap his little brain around the idea of
Thanking those who made him go to the end of the line
Or those who told him that he'd never amount to much
But his grandmother taught him to have the kind of faith
That you can't see or touch, so for his enemies
He continued to pray
Frankie's grandmother stressed that as long as
He responded the right way
He'd be one step closer to his destiny

The time was now nineteen seventy
His perfectly round shaped afro set the tone
It had nothing to do with style
But everything to do with growth, progression and increase
A black fist in the air replaced two fingers
That once symbolized peace
He found serenity within
And that inner peace translated to

A healthy dose of self-pride on the outside
He was happy that his grandmother was able to see
His maturation before she died
He owed it to her to make a difference before he met his maker
Frankie never asked for what he felt belonged to him
He was more of a taker
In his community, he became a mover and a shaker
But the powers that be would disagree

He fought to take his community back
It was nicknamed, "the city that sleeps with one eye open"
Because so many were addicted to crack
He knew that self-awareness
Was the only thing his people lacked
So, Frankie spearheaded a movement
He gathered up as many as he could
Who not only talked about change
But wanted to contribute to the improvement of the people
Frankie knew that before he could begin
The fight for equal rights
He had to rearrange the black mind state
Frankie had to teach them how to let negativity
Motivate them to do something positive
He wanted to make them cognitive of the fact
That the naysayers would never discourage them from being
Gangsters, killers and crooks
Because those occupations don't require textbooks

Black Pearls Before Swine

And knowledge is power
Frankie's people understood
And that wisdom began to breathe life
Back into the troubled neighborhood

But Frankie was at war with two enemies
The enemy within the neighborhood
Sharing the same color of skin
Who didn't want change because for so many years
They'd been profiteers
Selling poison to their own kind
And with the new frame of mind, inspired by Frankie
The dealers were losing money
And then the enemy on the exterior
Wanting to remain superior
Saw Frankie as a threat
His murder hasn't been solved yet

Frankie's legacy almost died, too
But there were many who didn't forget
To thank the naysayers in their prayers
And they became doctors, lawyers and mayors
Teachers, writers, leaders and musicians
All sharing the responsibility of continuing Frankie's mission

Keep Talking
(2011)

Keep talking with your sharp words
That cut straight to the soul
I won't let them take a toll on me
I am walking in purpose
And every onward step that I make
Your painful desire for my defeat seems to surface
But I abide
See me strut, watch me stride
Like a decorated warrior
I survived
And with this new life revived
I am a mightier force
And until my race is won
I will stay the course

Happiness
(2007)

Not on people
Nor on things
Should one depend
For it lies within thee
Happiness hates company
And independence
Should never render one
To be forsaken
For he is fulfilled
Who has taken
Responsibility

Never Give Up
(2011)

Even when the odds are stacked enormously high
And you feel that you'll never win
When everything around you has gone awry
There's triumph in the end

When it seems that all have counted you out
And your life takes a sudden twist
There's value in going the longer route
The reward's on the way, if you persist

Even if you fall a thousand times
Then get up, and fall once more
There'll always be hills and mountains to climb
And when it rains, it seems to pour

When your hopes and dreams are on delay
And you want to give up the fight
Don't let the troubles of yesterday
Poison your future and blurry your sight

Tracks
(2007)

My life has a soundtrack
'Cause I was born by the river
The crooked letter humpback to be exact
Rhythm and blues mixed with gospel
Sunday morning church pews
Let me know I was black
And that yes, Jesus loves me
Unlike my earthly father who hit the road like Jack
He wasn't fit for a family
Not with his city slick Chicago swagger
My pops was a rolling stone
But not like Mick Jagger
Because wherever he laid his hat was his home
Too much to comprehend for such a young dome
The next ten years, my mother, older sibling and I
Would roam back and forth from south to north
Exposed to things that were far from being pretty
We were living just enough for the city
And my mother would never accept pity
'Cause she was way too proud to beg or borrow
Pride is always the hardest thing to swallow
And where we lived, nothing seemed promising

Especially tomorrow
Sometimes it makes me wonder how we kept from going under

After playing the hand that we were dealt and coming up short
We made our way back to the Bible Belt
For a little moral support
I had to trade in jumping double dutch and playing hop scotch
For Jeopardy and Oprah
'Cause I was on my grandmother's watch
But I didn't mind one bit
Except for the smoke from all the cigarettes she lit
She would sit in her La-Z-Boy recliner
Needle, thread and fabric in hand
She was somewhat of a designer
Even at four, I was dressed in couture
Growing up around old folks made me much more mature
She used to tell me I was too grown
Ain't no sunshine since she been gone
Only dark clouds everyday
And divided we fell like a family that don't pray

We became strangers that favored
Never held anger towards my Savior
But the drop from middle class was humbling to say the least
We had to move to the side of town opposite of the east
Meanwhile, my brother had been devoured
In the belly of the beast

Black Pearls Before Swine

Mama was forced to wear a blue collar
Just to make a few dollars
This ain't living
Make me wanna holla and throw up both of my hands
I knew there had to be more to life
Than this current circumstance
And I wanted to explore
I used to dream so much that I'd forget that we were poor
But it was just my imagination running away
Though I had to maintain speed
'Cause if I ever lost the race against my mind
I'd forever be left behind

And I've encountered many roadblocks
On my way to find reason
Learned that people would enter my circle
For a lifetime or a season
I never dreamed he'd leave in summer
To escape the pain, I'd often fall into a deep slumber
He turned cold without admonition
Like winter under mid-July conditions
But spring came around and I came back to my senses
Preferred liberation over white picket fences
Independence helped me bid love good-bye
Maybe this is what it sounds like when doves cry
Never again would I put anyone before my dream
Decided to head out West

And discovered that things aren't always what they seem
The desire for lights, camera, action
Turned out to be a distraction from the true cause
And it's not for the applause or notoriety
The gift was put inside of me
To somehow make a useful contribution to society
And I'll share the experience, whether it is great
Or as small as an indistinct pearl
My life now has meaning to go along with this soundtrack
And I think to myself, what a wonderful world

Breaking Point
(2007)

Eyes losing perception
Back spineless and bruised
Head tilted in a downward direction
Feet nearly static and overused
Shoulders burdened by the heavy load
Mouth never inquiring why
Arms empty with nothing to hold
On both knees, with hands raised to the sky

The Future Is Watching
(2007)

The future is watching
So I carefully orchestrate each move I make
For the livelihood of a generation is at stake
And I want to see them soar

The future is watching
Seeing that I represent the very same environment
Living proof that where you've been is irrelevant
And opportunity knocks on every door

The future is watching
So I express sophistication with my style of dress
For respect is commanded in proper uniform
Resulting in success
And I want them to look the part

The future is watching
Seeing that I have a genuine concern
For the direction in which they'll turn
Knowing that someone cares makes them more eager to learn
And now the future is off to a promising start

NOTES

2.8 Great Migration] A movement of African-Americans between 1916 and 1970 from the rural south to northern cities (such as Chicago, New York, Detroit and Cleveland) . The goal was to escape discrimination and seek better economic opportunities. It is estimated that six million African-Americans relocated.

2.14 Harlem Renaissance] A literary and intellectual movement of the 1920's in which African-Americans excelled creatively, fostering a sense of racial pride and consciousness.

2.20 Zora] Zora Neal Hurston (1891-1960), was an African-American novelist, folklorist and anthropologist who played an integral part in the Harlem Renaissance. Hurston is known for having a vibrant personality and a strong desire to preserve black heritage. She penned the critically acclaimed 1937 novel, *Their Eyes Were Watching God*.

2.21 Louis] Louis Armstrong (1901-1971), trumpeter and singer, was one of the most influential jazz musicians of the Harlem Renaissance and helped to bring jazz to the mainstream. He is often cited as one of the first to scat sing, which is a form of singing using improvised melodies and rhythms, usually without words.

3.3 Emmet Till] Emmet Till was a 14 year-old African-American boy from Chicago who was killed in 1955 by two white men while visiting family in Mississippi. The men accused him of whistling at a white woman. They were charged with the crime, but acquitted soon after, which caused an uproar that led to the Civil Rights Movement.

5.4   Huey Newton]   Huey Newton (1942-1989), a social activist and one of the founding members of the Black Panther Party created in the 1960's to protect African-Americans from police brutality.

5.6   *ole man James*]   "Jim Crow" laws (1865-1965), robbed African-Americans of their basic human rights and enforced legal segregation.

8.6   Game and 'Ye]   Rappers, The Game and Kanye West's 2007 song titled, "You Wouldn't Get Far" criticizes video models and actresses on how they succeed in the entertainment business.

11.1   Medgar Evers]   Medgar Evers (1925-1963), was a Civil Rights Activist from Mississippi who organized boycotts of white owned companies that participated in discrimination of blacks. He also organized voter registrations and demonstrations. He was shot in front of his home by a white supremacist named Byron de la Beckwith.

18.2   Troy Davis]   Troy Davis (1968-2011), was an African-American man that was executed on September 21, 2011 for allegedly killing a white police officer. The case garnered national attention and outrage due to the lack of evidence against him.

40.2   Gloria Gaynor]   Gloria Gaynor is an African-American singer best known for her 1977 hit, "I Will Survive."

47.4   Seven and a crescent]   A seven and a crescent are components of the Nation of Gods and Earths (also known as the

Black Pearls Before Swine

Five Percent Nation) universal flag. The seven is a symbol of God and the crescent represents the moon, which is symbolic for women and wisdom.

49.2 Nat King Cole] Nat King Cole (1919-1965), was an African-American singer and jazz pianist who recorded the popular song "Unforgettable" in 1961.

50.6 Roy Hargrove] Roy Hargrove is a Grammy Award-winning African-American jazz trumpeter.

53.3 Ella] Ella Fitzgerald (1917-1996), was an African-American jazz vocalist known as the "First Lady of Jazz." She was the most popular female jazz vocalist in the U.S. for more than half a century.

71.2 Pacs and Scarfaces] Rappers, Tupac Shakur (1971-1996) and Scarface penned the 1997 hit, "Smile." The songs aim was to encourage those to smile in spite of it all. The appearance of Tupac Shakur was posthumous.

83.3 Crooked letter humpback] "M, I, crooked letter, crooked letter....humpback..." is an old southern verse children sang to help them learn to spell Mississippi.

84.4 Bible Belt] The Bible Belt is the southeastern region of the U.S. where Christianity is deeply rooted.

www.ingramcontent.com/pod-product-compliance
Lightning Source LLC
Chambersburg PA
CBHW061456040426
42450CB00008B/1382